ICE CREAM!

by JILL NEIMARK

Illustrated by Karen Milone-Dugan

HASTINGS HOUSE • PUBLISHERS

New York, NY 10016

For my grandparents, whose love of extravagant things,
from ice cream to cashmere to caviar, inspired this book

Library of Congress Cataloging in Publication Data
Neimark, Jill.
    Ice cream!
    Bibliography: p.
    Includes index.
    1. Ice cream, ices, etc. I. Milone-Dugan, Karen. II. Title.
TX795.N44   1986   641.8′62   84-10915
ISBN 0-8038-3440-3 tr. ed.
ISBN 0-8038-9290-X lib. ed.

Hastings House, Publishers
260 Fifth Avenue
New York, New York 10001

Distributed to the trade by:
Kampmann & Company, Inc.
New York, New York

Printed in the United States of America

Contents

Ice Cream:
The All-Time Treat

Imagine a burning hot day in the city of Rome about 2,000 years ago. The sun beats down like fire on the city's white stone roofs. Miles away, high in the mountains outside Rome, a man is running. He has a large bowl in his hands. As he runs up the steep slopes, he trips. But he jumps up to run again. The higher he goes, the cooler the air is. Finally he sees white patches. For high in the mountains the snow never melts. He stops and fills his bowl with heaps of the clean, cold snow. Then he begins to run back down the mountain. He knows he must go as fast as he can. Because he is a slave runner. And he is bringing the snow to the Emperor.

The Emperor's name is Nero. He is a man known far and wide for his cruelty. He likes to eat a frozen treat made of snow, fruit, wine and honey. In fact, he is so fond of this dessert that he has threatened to kill any slave runner who doesn't make it back to Rome before the snow in his bowl melts.

This is one story about the birth of the treat we
know today as ice cream. Not only has ice cream inspired emperors to kill, it has been flown on special
planes to soldiers during World War II. It has been a
favorite of many American presidents. George Washington used to make it himself in his own hand-cranked
machine. Thomas Jefferson had an 18-step recipe for
ice cream.

Hundreds of years ago, before ice cream was widely
known, the French king Louis XIV tricked his court with
it. At the end of a long feast his chef brought out eggs
in silver cups. Each guest was served one. They were
shocked that the king would serve such a plain, boring
dessert. But when they began to eat they found they
were tasting a sweet, cold, smooth treat that was nothing like an egg! It was shaped like an egg. But it was
really ice cream.

For a long time, ice cream was so rare a treat that only presidents, kings and queens were lucky enough to taste it. Now that we have electric ice cream machines and freezers, anybody can eat ice cream. And everybody does. We Americans gobble up more than 800 million gallons a year. That's enough to provide ten single-scoop cones for every human being on earth. And we don't stop there. We've invented endless flavors for our favorite treat—from vanilla to chocolate to ketchup ice cream, sauerkraut, peanut butter, and chili con-carne!

We've held ice cream eating contests. The world's

record went to Bennett D'Angelo. He wolfed down three pounds and six ounces in 90 seconds. That was in a town called Waltham, Massachusetts, in 1977, but ice cream eaters keep trying to beat him.

America also holds the record for the biggest sundae ever made. This ice-cream-lovers'-dream-come-true was created by the students at Michigan State University in 1982 (ingredients were donated by Friendly Ice Cream Corporation). It contained: 15,000 pounds of ice cream, 120 pounds of chocolate syrup, 25 pounds of Reese's Pieces, and 50 pounds of whipped topping.

In the name of ice cream, hundreds of Boston kids once marched on city hall. The year was 1921 and ice cream vendors had raised the price of a cone from five cents to a whopping ten cents. The kids were furious. They staged a protest and the vendors gave in.

Ice cream has actually made the fortune of many Americans. A cab driver named Steve opened his first ice cream store in 1973. Now he has stores throughout the Northeast. People line up around the block to buy his ice cream. In Vermont, two old pals named Ben and Jerry started an ice cream store in an old gas station. Ben and Jerry became a big success. In Washington D.C., Bob's Famous was started by a lawyer who got tired of law. Now senators and congresspeople drop in each day to buy a scoop of their favorite flavor.

Ice cream has come a long way since its first hot days in Rome. It has travelled from the Far East to Europe and America. Ice cream was once a rare treat for the rich. Now the U.S. government classes ice cream as an essential food. It has gone from a few flavors to hundreds upon hundreds.

America consumes more ice cream than any other country. Every night, all over America, even in the darkest and coldest winter storm, kids and adults wait in line to buy ice cream. On crowded city streets and on quiet country roads, at home and in the ice cream parlor, there is enough for every ice cream fanatic.

Here, just sample a few . . . Try chocolate cinnamon raisin. Fresh crushed strawberry. Rich and chewy oreo mint. Vanilla fit for a king. How about chocolate fudge? Or chocolate cheesecake? Bittersweet chocolate, perhaps. Or chocolate chocolate chip. Sugar plum, nutcracker sweet, or creamy banana mango. Pistachio that just melts in your mouth. One scoop, please. No, how about two scoops? Actually, a gallon sounds just fine . . .

No one knows just how Nero's snow dessert was made. But this is an age-old recipe that's probably pretty close to his.

Fruit Snow

2 cups fresh, clean snow
¼ cup grape juice (or any kind of juice you like)
1 tablespoon honey

Put the snow in a bowl, trying not to pack it down. Mix grape juice and honey and pour evenly over the snow. Eat it immediately, before it melts!   *Serves 4.*

2

How Ice Cream Grew Up

No one will ever know who really invented ice cream. We do know that in the year 1295, an Italian named Marco Polo tasted ice cream during his travels in the Far East. He returned to Venice with tales of the exotic milk sherbets he had eaten in China. Soon the Italians were making their own. The new treat was a sensation, although only the rich got to taste it.

Years later ice cream was still going strong. The Medicis, a wealthy family that ruled Italy for many years, loved ice cream. They created their own special recipes. And in 1533, Catherine de Medici married King Henry of France and brought him her royal recipes. She included a recipe for ice cream. Soon the French people were clamoring for the sweet, cool confection.

From France, ice cream travelled to Germany and England. When English colonists came to America they brought recipes for ice cream with them. But back in those days, most Americans got to taste about a teaspoon of ice cream a year. The treat was rare and hard

11

to make. First, you had to find some ice—in a frozen river or stream or high in the mountains—since no one had invented the freezer yet. Once you had your ice, you mixed some cream and fruit in a pot. Then you had to beat the cream by hand and shake it up and down in a second pot of salt and ice. The salt and ice kept the first pot cold. Beat and shake—up and down—round and round. Finally, you ended up with ice cream.

Around 1800, some clever Americans began to harvest ice. In the winter, they would chop and saw blocks of ice from frozen rivers and lakes. They would ship the ice to ice houses. These houses were actually man-made caves lined with bricks, with a small opening. The ice was dropped through the hole and it was so cold inside that the ice melted very, very slowly. It usually lasted through the summer.

As a result, people could eat ice cream year round. The dessert became more and more popular. Ice cream was served at the White House and in the streets. Vendors went around with horse and buggy, yelling, "I Scream, Ice Cream!" Others carried special tin cans of ice cream on their shoulders, laughing and singing songs about ice cream. They were called the "Ice Scream Men."

In the 1830's, ice-making machines were invented. Though they were often crude, they made ice even easier to get. Then, in 1846, a woman named Nancy Johnson changed the fate of ice cream. She invented a hand-cranked ice cream maker. It meant you no longer had to beat ice cream with a wooden spoon. You didn't have to shake it up and down in a pot of ice. You simply turned a crank.

Catherine de Medici had her own special recipes for ice cream.

The ice cream maker was a big hit. It showed up in American homes everywhere. Thousands of boys and girls—some of them our own grandparents and parents—grew up cranking out their own silky, rich, cool, sweet homemade ice cream. Sometimes they went into their backyards and picked peaches or pears or berries and mixed those in, too. Even today some people claim that nothing compares with hand-cranked ice cream. It's still a lot of work, though. The hand-cranked machine you use at home is almost exactly the same as it was decades ago, when it was first invented. It takes about an hour to churn out ice cream by hand. But many people feel it's worth the trouble. Some professional chefs, for instance, wouldn't consider serving anything but their own hand-cranked ice cream delights. To those chefs, and the lucky people who eat their treats, store-bought ice cream just doesn't compare.

In fact, most ice cream was made by hand at home until 1851. Then, almost by accident, the commercial ice cream business got started. One day a milk dealer in Baltimore, Maryland saw that his dairy was making too much cream. His name was Jacob Fussell, and he had been selling milk for years. But he couldn't sell all of his cream. He couldn't store it, either. The only thing to do with it, he decided, was make ice cream out of it.

Before he knew it, Jacob's ice cream was selling like mad. He was making so much ice cream that he stopped selling milk and turned his dairy plant into an ice cream factory. Soon he was opening ice cream factories in other cities.

Jacob's success was only the beginning. Other men opened ice cream factories. New developments helped ice cream along, as well. With the wider use of electricity came electric ice cream makers. These machines made more ice cream, a lot faster. When the refrigerator was invented, ice cream no longer had to be stored in cold boxes of salt and ice. Instead, it was kept in huge freezers. Soon after, condensed and dry milk were perfected. Both could be kept for long periods. Many ice cream manufacturers used them along with fresh milk and cream.

In 1895 the pasteurizing machine was introduced. It sterilized milk, killing germs and bacteria that, until then, had sometimes made people sick. Milk—and ice cream—was now safer to eat and drink. And just a few years later, in 1899, the process of homogenization was invented. It helped break up the fat particles in milk and made it easier to digest. It gave ice cream a creamier, smoother texture.

All these new machines made a difference. But the single most important invention came in 1926. Scientists perfected a machine called the "continuous freezer." With it, ice cream could be mass produced.

The freezer seemed to work like magic compared to the old methods. It is still used today, and it produces a continuous stream of ice cream in just a few seconds.

How does it work? Its vital part is a nickel tube about three feet long and eight inches wide. This tube has two walls. In between those two walls is liquid ammonia. The ammonia is terribly cold—about 22° F. It keeps the inside wall of the tube just as cold. Ammonia can be kept at that temperature without freezing. This is why it is used instead of cold water which freezes at 32° F and does not get much colder.

The ice cream mix is pumped through the tube

under great pressure. There are blades inside the tube that whip the ice cream as it is pumped through. As soon as the liquid ice cream hits the metal blades, it begins to freeze. The great pressure, the cold, and the turning blades work together to make ice cream in a few seconds flat. It shoots out the other end into big containers. These containers are brought to a bitterly cold room, where the temperature is never more than $-10°F$. The ice cream is left there to harden.

With the help of this new machine the big ice cream craze began. People could buy ice cream in drugstores, from trucks, in the streets, in distant mountain towns, on farms, and in cities. Other countries fell in love with the dessert all over again. The Japanese, who are very fond of tea, invented many tea ice creams that are still

popular today. They are served in Japanese restaurants all over the world. In the Philippines they made ice cream from native fruits like the star apple and *ube*, a kind of yam. In India they made mango ice cream.

Ice cream became a part of many different Americans' lives. People spread it on their toast in the morning instead of butter. People gave parties in the spring called ice cream socials. In the 1920s during the Prohibition era, drinking wine or beer or any kind of liquor was against the law. Thousands of Americans drank ice cream sodas instead. After school, after the movies, on weekends, and almost every single night, teenagers flocked to the soda fountain at the drugstore.

One of the very few places where it wasn't so easy to get ice cream was—prison. A convict called Lawson

D. "Two Quart" Butler found this especially irksome. Lawson got his middle name because he could wolf down two quarts of ice cream in one sitting. "Two Quart" escaped from prison once, and the F.B.I. was after him. Most escaped convicts head for a safe hiding place just as quickly as they can, but not "Two Quart." He had something important to do first: he wanted some ice cream. A crowd gathered to watch him eat his usual two quarts. He must have eaten fast, because by the time the police got there, "Two Quart" was gone. As the story goes, when he was finally caught, Lawson said he'd be happy to go back to prison, if he could just get his two quarts a day.

Ice cream became so popular that many people began to sell it illegally. They were called bootleggers. They cranked out their own ice cream and passed it off as a famous brand. In March and April of 1933, 899 ice cream bootleggers were arrested!

From 1900 to 1978, the amount of ice cream made in America increased 160 times. At first, most ice cream was served in restaurants and in drugstore soda fountains. But in the 1950's, soda fountains began to fall out of favor. Drugstore owners began to remove them—perhaps because they learned they could make more money selling other products. Ice cream needed a new home.

It found one in supermarkets, where long freezers began to stock up gallon after gallon of ice cream. It sold quickly. Some people in the ice cream business decided that if ice cream cost less, it would sell even more. They began to put in less cream and more milk. That helped lower the cost. Sometimes they used artificial ingredients, because they too were cheaper. The price of ice cream for many years was about 59¢ for a whole gallon.

Meanwhile, many ice cream makers were hard at work inventing new flavors. In the 1930s, Howard Johnson's, the famous restaurant chain, unveiled their "28 flavors." They were a sensation. Most everyone had been selling just vanilla, chocolate and strawberry. Suddenly you could go out to lunch and order something as special as Peppermint Stick.

Many other flavors have been invented over the years. But even today, vanilla is still the world's favorite flavor. Chocolate runs a close second, and strawberry is third. Each part of the country seems to have its own passion. Crushed peach has always been a hit in the South. Coffee ice cream is a favorite in New England. New York likes its coffee ice cream strong. Boston likes it mild. Butter pecan is the hands-down winner in Texas. Californians go wild over date and prune ice creams—but those two flavors almost never sell anywhere else.

In recent years, several cousins of ice cream have become popular. One is frozen yogurt, which is more tart than ice cream and has less calories. Another tasty invention is soy ice cream, which is made from soybeans. It contains no milk or butterfat so it is often eaten by people who are allergic to milk products. It often goes by the name of Tofutti. It contains only 128 calories per four-ounce scoop, where gourmet ice creams contain about 325 calories. And it tastes good.

Today the average American hoards about four pints of ice cream in the home freezer. More than half the ice cream slurped here is a snack—not a mealtime dessert. A food critic named Gael Greene sums it up: "I shall never trust anyone who doesn't love ice cream." Most of us would probably agree.

Here's our third President's special recipe for vanilla ice cream, just as he wrote it in his personal cookbook. As you see, in the 1700's making ice cream was very complicated.

Thomas Jefferson's
Recipe for Vanilla Ice Cream

2 bottles of good cream
6 egg yolks
½ pound of sugar
1 stick of vanilla

Mix the yolks and sugar. Put the cream on a fire in a casserole, first putting in a stick of vanilla.

When near boiling, take it off and pour gently into the mixture of eggs and sugar.

Stir it well.

Put it on the fire again, stirring it thoroughly with a spoon to prevent it from sticking to the casserole.

When near boiling, take it off and strain it through a towel.

Put it in an ice pail.

Then set it in ice an hour before it is to be served. Put into the ice a handful of salt.

Put ice all around the ice pail—a layer of ice and a layer of salt, for 3 layers.

Put salt on the cover of the ice pail and cover the whole with ice.

Leave it for a quarter of an hour.

Then turn the ice pail in the ice for ten minutes.

Open the ice pail to loosen the ice cream from the inside of the pail. Close it and continue to turn the pail.

When ice cream is ready, stir it well with the spoon. Put it in molds. Put it back in ice until the moment of serving it.

Immerse the mold in warm water, until the ice cream comes out. Serve it on a plate.

3

The Ice Cream Revolution

The story of ice cream is also the story of many wonderful inventions. Like the ice cream soda, flowing over with foam and topped with mounds of whipped cream. Or the ice cream cone, invented by accident at the 1904 St. Louis World's Fair. Or ice cream on a stick, which made Good Humor famous.

It's hard to imagine a time when ice cream sodas weren't around. But in October of 1874 no one had heard or dreamed of such a dessert. A man named Robert Green was selling soda-and-sweet-cream drinks at his outdoor stand in Philadelphia. He'd pour a little cream in the bottom of a glass, add soda and stir it up.

Suddenly he ran out of cream. When his next customer came by asking for soda and cream, he put in some vanilla ice cream instead. Robert was probably as surprised as anybody when people started demanding his new invention. His sales soared from $6 a day to $600 a day. He went on to open an ice cream soda business.

We didn't always have ice cream sundaes either. Nobody can be sure who first got the idea of pouring syrup over ice cream. But we can guess why the sundae was invented and how it got its name. Many American towns in the 1890s were very religious. They felt Sunday was a holy day, meant only for rest and quiet. It's hard to believe now, but they actually passed laws against serving ice cream sodas on Sunday.

Never on Sunday.

People may have thought that by passing a law against ice cream sodas, which were so popular, they would put an end to all the kids and adults hanging out in the drugstore on Sunday. But, one story goes, there was a clever drugstore owner in Evanston, Illinois. He thought long and hard about the "Sunday Soda Menace." If sodas were against the law, he wasn't going to serve them; but no one had thought to pass a law against ice cream! He came up with a clever idea. He poured the soda syrup over ice cream in a dish, and

called it an "Ice Cream Sunday." It caught on. Other drugstore owners copied him. But, just to be safe, they decided not to use the word "Sunday" for a sweet treat. They might get in trouble all over again! So they changed the spelling to "Sundae". And by 1900 sundaes were a national favorite.

But an even bigger treat was in store for ice cream lovers. Someone was about to invent the ice cream cone.

The fellow's name was Ernest Hamwi. He had come all the way from Syria to America in 1903. In 1904 he joined the World's Fair in St. Louis, Missouri. He was selling a Persian dessert called *Zalabia*. It was a thin pastry baked on a waffle iron, and served with sugar and other sweets.

Mr. Hamwi's stand happened to be right next to an ice cream stand. Everyone seemed to want ice cream. Mr. Hamwi watched the customers coming and going.

THE CONE
STANDS
ALONE

THE
SPIRAL

FOR THE
SLOW
EATER

THE
50
SCOOPER

In fact, the ice cream sold so well that one day the stand ran out of dishes for the treat.

Mr. Hamwi lost no time. He rolled one of his wafers into the shape of a cone. He let it cool and harden. Then he offered it to the ice cream man, who quickly filled it up.

It was a stroke of genius. The customers loved it. There were fifty ice cream booths at the fair, and pretty soon they were all selling ice cream cones. The cone was such a big hit that even before the fair was over, the town of St. Louis had designed special molds for baking the cone.

Mr. Hamwi soon founded the Missouri Cone Company. Ovens were built for baking the waffles. Workers rolled them by hand into cones. Then a young student in Ohio designed a machine that rolled the cone mechanically. Today, millions of cones are rolled out on these machines. They work so fast that they can make 150,000 cones a day.

The cone was so popular that for many years companies kept trying to invent new shapes for it. They made cones that stood up alone, cones with spirals, cones with basins to catch dripping ice cream, big cones, small cones. But today the cone is still pretty much the same as Mr. Hamwi's and billions of them are eaten each year.

In 1919, a candy store owner named Christian Nelson came up with another big ice cream invention. He decided vanilla ice cream would be even better covered with a thin layer of chocolate. At first he couldn't get the chocolate to stick to the ice cream. It just slid right off. But then he added cocoa butter to the chocolate, and it worked. Nelson was overjoyed.

He called his new treat the "I-Scream Bar", but his creation was a failure. No one bought it. He had almost given up on the idea when he met Russell Stover. Russell was in the ice cream business. He joined up with Christian and renamed the bar the "Eskimo Pie." The name made a tremendous difference. The first 250,000 Eskimo Pies sold out in 24 hours. By 1922, people were eating a million pies a day. Today there are many copies of the Eskimo Pie. Even so, the company reports that Americans eat 750 million of their pies each year.

Meanwhile, Harry Burt, who had invented a lollipop called the "Good Humor Sucker," heard about Eskimo Pies. He decided to try and make his own. When he tested it on his family, his daughter asked why he didn't put the bar on a stick, just like his Good Humor Lollipop.

It was another stroke of genius. Harry started selling his Good Humor Ice Cream Sucker in a white truck. He put bells from the family sled on the truck. The truck rolled through town, ringing merrily. Kids ran to meet it and buy Good Humor ice cream.

Another invention that swept America was the Dixie Cup. The Dixie was a small cup of ice cream that cost only a nickel. Each cup had a paper lid with a picture on the inside. There were pictures of animals, movie stars, cowboys, American heroes, and baseball stars. Kids collected and traded the lids. The Dixie craze spread across America. It lasted nearly twenty-five years. Today some of the lids are collector's items. They sell for as much as $25 a piece.

What about the ice cream sandwich, you may be wondering? Who invented that? And the banana split? And the ice cream float? We don't know precisely when and where they began. Well then, you may ask, what about the ice cream scoop? It goes back to the turn of the century. And ice cream makers have been trying to improve it ever since. Baskin-Robbins uses a method called wax-casting to make its scoops. It was used long ago by sculptors. First a scoop is made out of wax. It is dipped in sand, and then in gravel, and then in paste, and in a few other solutions. This strange mix hardens on the wax. Then the wax is melted out, and just the hardened mix is left. This becomes the "mold". Molten steel is poured into it. It dries. Then a man comes along with a huge hammer. He hits it very hard. The metal scoop falls out, ready to use!

Scooping ice cream is itself a complicated matter. Today, at most ice cream parlors, scoopers are trained. They must roll the scoop in a special way to get a strip of ice cream that curls around itself. And they must dish out an equal amount in each scoop, or customers would complain.

Ice cream comes to us in many forms. It comes inside chocolate, in sandwiches, and hiding under layers of nuts and fruit. We have metal molds to make ice cream turkeys at Thanksgiving, ice cream hearts on Valentine's Day, and ice cream Santas at Christmas. We use ice cream flowers and leaves at weddings. We've invented ice cream cakes, ice cream bon-bons, and ice cream pastries. One ice cream maker has even come up with ice cream spaghetti (he uses grated coconut instead of parmesan cheese). That may sound like the limit, but somebody's bound to top it soon.

Here's an ice cream soda that's been a big hit for years.

Black Cow

Vanilla ice cream
Whipped cream
Root beer

Fill a glass ¾ full with root beer. Add two scoops of vanilla ice cream. Top with whipped cream. Slurp!

4

Big-Time Ice Cream

What's so special about ice cream, anyway? Take some milk, some cream, some sugar, and a few other ingredients, and you've got it. Simple. Or is it?

Not really. Not if you're making big-time ice cream—ice cream for sale. There are many different approaches, and countless ingredients. And there are very few rules and standards. The government requires that ice cream contain at least 10% butterfat and weigh 4.5 pounds per gallon. That's about it. The National Association of Ice Cream Manufacturers has been fighting the government since the group was founded in 1900. And so far they have been winning. They do not have to list all their ingredients on ice cream cartons.

Well, how many ingredients can there be, after all, you may ask? More than you might think! Here are just a few of the things that may turn up in your average supermarket brand ice cream:

Milk	Honey
Skim Milk	Corn sweeteners
Buttermilk	Locust bean
Butter	Corn syrup
Butter oil	Maltose syrup
Nonfat dry milk	Fructose
Condensed milk	Eggs
Evaporated milk	Frozen eggs
Powdered whey	Powdered eggs
Malted milk	Salt
Cream	Artificial coloring
Frozen Cream	Nuts
Sugar	Fruit
Beet sugar	Frozen fruit
Sucrose	Dried fruit
Brown sugar	Artificial flavorings

In addition, many ice creams contain two other kinds of ingredients. They are called *emulsifiers* and *stabilizers*. Emulsifiers hold ice cream together, and keep it from becoming runny. The most common emulsifiers are monoglycerides, diglycerides, and polysorbate. Stabilizers help prevent ice cream from forming crystals and tasting grainy. The most common stabilizers are guar gum, cellulose, and alginite gum.

Of course, ice cream wasn't always made with emulsifiers and stabilizers. Commercial ice cream makers began to use them because they wanted their ice cream to last a long time, and to taste smooth and creamy even after it had been shipped many miles. But the emulsifiers and stabilizers most often used in ice cream are generally safe, according to the Center for Science in the Public Interest.

How is most commercial ice cream made? There are two types of common freezers. One is the batch freezer, which takes up to eight minutes to make just one five-gallon batch of ice cream. The batch freezer is most often used by small shops that make their own ice cream on the spot. The continuous freezer is the one used by most large commercial ice cream manufacturers. It makes ice cream in less than 60 seconds. First the liquids—the cream, milk and syrup—are put in a large vat and heated. Then the dry solids—powdered milk, dried egg yolk, stabilizers and emulsifiers—are added. When the mix is very hot (about 120°F), sugar is added. Next the mix is pasteurized (to destroy germs and bacteria), and then homogenized. You may remember from Chapter Two that homogenization breaks up the particles of fat and blends them through the milk.

The hot mix is now cooled to nearly freezing—about 32°F. Flavors are added. The mix is pumped through the turning blades of the continuous freezer machine. As it shoots through, it freezes instantly and turns to ice cream. Last, the finishing touches—fruit, nuts, or candies—are added.

Temperature is extremely important. The ice cream must be kept at about −10°F to stay hard and smooth. It must be kept that cold while it is shipped and when it reaches the store. If the ice cream melts a little and then freezes over again, it will develop icy crystals, will taste a little bit sandy, and may shrink.

One important ingredient in ice cream is something that may surprise you: *air*. Air makes a huge difference in the richness, creaminess, and weight of ice cream. Every ice cream maker puts air into ice cream. The blades of the freezing machine whip air bubbles into the mix. Although ice cream must weigh at least 4.5 pounds per gallon, even an ice cream that's half air (50%) can meet the weight requirement. Homemade ice cream, and some expensive "gourmet" brands often weigh about twice that amount. Pick up a gallon of the most expensive store-bought ice cream and you'll be lugging eight pounds of cream, sugar, eggs *and* 20% air home to eat! Some brands of ice cream use as little as 9% air. But if no air were added to your ice cream, you would end up chewing a dessert that tasted like sweet, heavy ice cubes.

Another secret of the ice cream industry is the
amount of butterfat used. Butterfat is the fat that is
present in milk and milk products (like cream, cheese,
butter, and ice cream). All ice creams are required by
law to include at least 10% butterfat. But the more expensive brands often use about 16% butterfat in their
mix. That extra 6% can make a big difference. When
we say that an ice cream tastes "rich" that usually means
it's high in butterfat. Some people wonder why no one
has invented an ice cream that is, say, . . . 50% butterfat! Or 75%. The reason is that most everyone who tries

to use much more than 16% butterfat ends up churning out a gallon of—guess what?—butter!

A few different ingredients are what separates ice cream from other frozen desserts. Frozen custard is similar to ice cream, but it contains more egg yolk—about 1.4%. Ice milk is also similar, but it contains less butterfat—between 2% and 7%. It has fewer calories, too.

Sherbet is also a popular dessert. It contains milk, sugar, fruits and fruit juices. But it only has about 1% or 2% fat. Water ices, which are very popular, contain no milk at all.

The age-old recipe for Italian ice cream—*Gelato*—has found fans across America. Using a special method, its makers whip in only 9% air and just enough butterfat to meet American standards (10%), but still achieve a rich, creamy taste.

Some like ice cream as heavy and full of butterfat as they can get it. Others prefer it light and airy. In 1981, *Time* magazine reported a contest run by food experts. They tested 28 vanilla ice creams. None of the judges knew which ice cream they were tasting. They just closed their eyes, tasted, and ranked each one. The results were surprising. Some of our most expensive ice creams ended far down on the list. The hands-down winner was an inexpensive carton of low-butterfat vanilla ice cream called Kiss, which sells in supermarkets.

Like milk, ice cream contains protein, calcium, phosphorus and vitamin A, although in different amounts. It has twice the calories and fat that milk has, but it is still less fattening than many other desserts. A half-cup of supermarket ice cream is about 180 calo-

ries, and a half cup of the heaviest vanilla ice cream is 263 calories. But that's still not as bad as a slice of apple pie, which is a hundred calories more.

In the last ten years, more and more brands of ice cream have been made with old-fashioned ingredients. Instead of dried milk or corn sweeteners or artificial flavors, they contain whole cream, eggs, fresh fruits and natural flavorings. Sometimes these ice creams have imported ingredients—like bits of Swiss chocolate. Because fresh and imported ingredients cost more, these ice creams are expensive, but the people who buy them feel they taste better.

Natural ice creams have been inspiring natural ice cream cones. Instead of using mass-produced cones, some stores now make their own cones on waffle irons— just like in the old days. They pour homemade batter onto the waffle irons, let them heat to a crisp texture and roll each cone by hand.

Even so, the dairies that make the basic supermarket brands across the country are still supplying two-thirds of America's ice cream. They churn out millions of gallons for supermarkets. Some dairies make their own brands as well.

Most ice cream is produced within 800 miles of

where it is sold. That's because it's expensive to move ice cream. It has to be packed in ice at very cold temperatures. One mistake in temperature in the factory can cost tens of thousands of dollars and a whole lot of ice cream can go to ruin.

In ice cream factories, freezers are washed and cleaned daily. The freezer parts must be left to dry in the air—not dried with towels or cloth. This prevents germs in the towels from contaminating the parts. Ice cream mix is never stored at temperatures over 40°F or exposed to sunlight. Even though 40°F feels cold to human beings, it allows bacteria to grow by the thousands.

Making ice cream is an art and an industry. There are those who will always insist that homemade, hand-cranked ice cream tastes best. Some want only the most expensive store-bought brands made with natural ingredients. Others like nothing better than to dig into a carton of fluffy, smooth vanilla from the supermarket. It may have twenty or thirty ingredients, it may have been heated, cooled, pumped through machines, stored at freezing temperatures, shipped across several states, and contain 50% air—but it still tastes good.

Here is a recipe for strawberry ice cream. You can make it without an ice cream machine.

Strawberry Ice Cream

3 eggs
3 cups strawberries (fresh or frozen)
1½ cups sugar
1½ cups whipping cream

Separate the egg yolks from the egg whites.

If you're using fresh strawberries, wash them and cut off stems and bad spots. Put the berries in a bowl and mash them with a big spoon or fork, or blend them in a blender or food processor. Put the berries into a strainer over a bowl. Take a wooden spoon and press the strawberries through the strainer. Set the bowl aside.

In a large bowl beat the egg yolks until thick and creamy. Beat in the sugar and whipping cream. Beat until the mix is thick enough to form soft peaks. Stir in the strawberries.

In another bowl, beat the egg whites until frothy. Stir the egg whites into the strawberry mixture. Pour into a 9-inch square pan, cover with tin foil, and place in freezer until firm, about 4 hours. *Serves 8.*

5

Name Your Flavors

Mocha Polka. Lox and Bagels. Cactus Candy. Yankee Doodle Strudel. Bob's Kahlua. Mountain High. Vanilla and chocolate chips and butterscotch chips and pecans and crushed Reese's peanut butter cups and crumbled Oreo cookies and raisins—and more. (Is that a flavor?) Well, it's actually called a "mix-in"—your favorite candies, cookies and flavorings are ground up and mixed right in with your ice cream. Steve's ice cream stores in the East specialize in "mix-ins" and other stores serve them too.

American ice cream makers have had a lot of fun inventing flavors. Baskin-Robbins is the leader, with over 500 flavors at this very moment. The dairy school at Ohio State University made headlines in almost every paper in the country when they came up with Brassicaceous (horseradish and root-beer) ice cream. They also created Mustard Delight. And Sauerkraut Sherbet. One company hoped to win the hearts of Americans with

41

yellow tomato ice cream. That was in the 1930's. No one bought it. But dill-pickle ice cream sells well in Michigan, where it was invented. And in Arizona, a fiery hot pepper ice cream has its fans.

Imagine spending your life trying to think up new flavors for ice cream. You would be a flavor scientist. You might have gone to one of the famous dairy schools. Michigan State, Pennsylvania State, Ohio State, and other universities have programs in "food science." There you can learn how to make milk, cheese, ice cream and many other foods and desserts. You might spend many long nights trying to invent a sweet potato ice cream, or a better banana. You might later go to work for one of the big ice cream companies, and spend your days tasting and creating different flavors.

It sounds like fun. But no matter what flavor you created, you probably couldn't beat America's favorite—vanilla. It forms the base for all other flavors. The standard vanilla ice cream contains cream, sugar, eggs and real vanilla beans. Vanilla beans are almost black in color. They leave little black flecks in the ice cream. Some fans don't realize this. There are many people who have sent back a fine vanilla ice cream because they thought the flecks were dirt!

Take a look at some cherry ice cream one day. Don't those bright red cherries look scrumptious? The truth is, if they are bright red they have been bleached white and then dyed red! In the more expensive (and, say their makers, the best) cherry ice creams the cherries are untouched. That means they are dark red or black. They don't look as pretty. But they taste just as good.

The most natural mint ice cream is not green, either. Natural mint flavor is clear. And the best peach

ice cream uses overripe peaches—the kind you would never eat if you found them on your kitchen table!

The one company that has brought us the most—and some of the most surprising—ice cream flavors is Baskin-Robbins. They've tried almost everything, from ketchup ice cream to ninety kinds of chocolate.

Someone—a child or an adult—may send a flavor suggestion in the mail. More often, the flavor is invented at Baskin-Robbins' own laboratory in Burbank, California. There lab technicians in white coats make, measure, test and store ice cream. The flavors are tested out on marketing people.

Many of the flavors never make it past the test panel. The lab has tested and rejected flavors like Chop Suey, Rum N' Coke, Bacon Ripple, Dandelion Wine, Liver N' Onions, Potato Chip, Clam Nectar, and Hot Cross Bun. Others that *did* make it were failures. For example, Goody-Goody Gumdrop was dropped when the tiny, frozen gumdrops chipped some teeth.

Other flavors have become classics. Remember Jamoca Almond Fudge? Or Pralines 'N Cream? Once they were just another idea in a lab technician's head.

The laboratory has some amazing methods for making their flavors. Did you ever wonder about chocolate chip ice cream? Do they stir those tiny chips in by hand? No! The ice cream is pumped through a container. As it passes through, it is blasted with melted, semi-sweet chocolate. When the hot, liquid chocolate hits the freezing cold ice cream it hardens, shatters and explodes—into thousands of tiny chocolate chips.

Other companies work hard at creating flavors as well. In Chicago, Bresler's Ice Cream boasts over 200 flavors. They created Iced Tea ice cream, and a delicious bittersweet chocolate. Good Humor still offers new flavors each year. They've brought us Watermelon ice, Gingerbread, and many other unique flavors. In the East, Breyer's Ice Cream offers only twelve flavors at a time. They've been working on their flavors since 1866. And sometimes it can be frustrating. According to *Time* magazine, Breyer's found that a blend of pumpkin and squash tasted better than plain old pumpkin. But they knew nobody was going to buy "Pumpkin and Squash" ice cream. It just didn't sound right. So they had to work harder on pure pumpkin.

Some ice cream makers don't worry about inventing new flavors. They just work on the old favorites. One famous cookiemaker, David Liederman of David's Cookies, puts imported Swiss chocolate in his ice cream. Another brand, Gelato Modo, makes ices which are 85% fresh fruit. And, all around the country, Americans create their own special recipes, whether it's for simple vanilla, and chocolate, or way-out flavors like eggnog-pumpkin pie, or tangerine-chip, or coconut-cashew . . .

Inventing Your Own Flavors

Vanilla ice cream
Any ingredients you like—tiny pieces of fruit, nuts, syrups, spices, cake or cookie crumbs, cereals, candies, peanut butter, coconut—use your imagination!

Put some vanilla ice cream in a bowl. Quickly and gently mix in two or three ingredients. Eat immediately. (If you refreeze your ice cream, remember that some ingredients—like fruit—may freeze very hard.)

6

Ice Cream Wars

People who eat ice cream are always ready to argue that their favorite brand of ice cream is the "best." But the people who make ice cream get into fights too—big ones.

Remember the ice cream bar called the Eskimo Pie? It was the very first one, but soon dozens of imitations showed up. Eventually the inventors were spending $4,000 a day on lawsuits to protect their idea. They almost went broke, even though they were selling a million pies a day. Russell Stover, one of the partners, got so upset he sold his share in the business, and went off to open a candy store. (Stover's candy stores have since become famous.)

One amazing ice cream war was launched by Reuben Mattus, who invented Häagen-Dazs. At the age of 12 he was squeezing lemons for the family business. He and his mother delivered lemon ices to people in the Bronx, in New York. They rode in a horse-drawn cart. They were doing well. But then the big businesses

started cutting their prices, and the Mattus family couldn't keep up.

By 1960, U.S. supermarkets were selling ice cream like lightning at 69¢ a gallon. Mattus was in deep trouble. So he did the one thing the big companies couldn't afford to do.

He made a gourmet ice cream. It had lots of butterfat and very little air. It was very expensive. It only came in small pint containers. Strangest of all, it had a funny, nonsense name. The name was really just a jumble of letters. But customers didn't know that. They picked up a pint of the new treat. They saw a map of Scandinavia on the lid. So they thought the ice cream was imported from Europe.

A lot of big companies laughed at Reuben Mattus. Why would anyone pay twice as much money for a pint of a funny-sounding ice cream instead of a gallon of their own brand?

They stopped laughing when Reuben started selling 50 million pints of ice cream a year. That's when the war began. One big American food company teamed up with an uncle of Reuben's and made their own gourmet ice cream. They decided to use a foreign sounding name, too. They called it Früsen Gladjé. That means "frozen delight" in Swedish. Where was their ice cream made? In upstate New York. Another "import" came along as well. It was called Alpen Zauber—which means "alpine magic" in German. It was produced in Brooklyn, New York.

Häagen-Dazs tried to sue Früsen Gladjé. Alpen Zauber tried to sue Häagen-Dazs. Meanwhile, all three companies were selling ice cream hand over fist. All three were making money! And before long *new* brands of gourmet ice cream were popping up all over the country.

Each ice cream company believes their product is the best there is. (And each company has plenty of customers who agree.) Doris Mattus, Reuben (Häagen-Dazs)

Mattus' wife, says, "Once our customers taste Häagen-Dazs, we've got them for life!" According to *Time* magazine, Tom Carvel, owner of Carvel's ice cream, scoffs. He says the country's best is his own, which is made fresh each day. Breyer's ice cream laughs at the rest. Breyer's has been known to claim that in one week they sell more of their ice cream than Häagen-Dazs sells across America in a year. And Baskin-Robbins simply points out that they do much more than sell ice cream. As their slogan claims, "We make people happy."

In spite of all the ice cream wars, ice cream is one of the happiest stories in American business. For in the ice cream business the giants flourish—and so does the single person cranking out a homemade treat. Dart & Kraft makes both Sealtest and Breyer's ice cream, and is in first place, selling nearly $340 million worth of ice cream a year. But there's still room for Borden, and Sedutto's, and Good Humor, and Howard Johnson's, and Ben and Jerry's, and Friendly's and Bassett's, and Swensen's, and others. There's still room for Mayfield's in Tennessee, Lickety Split in Denver, and Graeter's in Cincinnati. There's still room for you!

A Taste-Test Party

Buy several brands of the same flavor, including supermarket and gourmet ice creams. Invite some friends over. Label the bottoms of your ice cream dishes with the names of the brands. Fill the dishes, mix them up, and start sampling. You may be surprised at how different the same flavor can taste. See if everyone (or anyone) can agree on the best-tasting ice cream.

7

Ice Cream Treats You Can Make

You can make your own ice cream at home. You can invent your own flavor. You can create new ice cream treats. Who knows, you might even become famous!

There are several ways to make ice cream. You can buy a hand-cranked ice cream maker or an electric one. Or you can simply mix some delicious ingredients together and freeze them.

With your own ice cream maker you can usually produce up to a gallon of ice cream at a time. All ice cream makers come with directions. To use one you will need salt and ice cubes. This mix of salt and ice is known as brine. It helps freeze the ice cream.

Here is a recipe you can make with either an electric or a hand-cranked ice cream maker. You can make all the other recipes in this chapter without an ice cream machine.

Chocolate and Marshmallow Ice Cream

⅓ cup unsweetened cocoa powder
1 cup sugar
2 cups milk
1 teaspoon vanilla extract
⅛ teaspoon salt
2 cups whipping cream
2 squares semisweet chocolate
1 cup tiny marshmallows

Mix the cocoa powder and the sugar in a saucepan. Pour in the milk, a little at a time, and mix well. Then stir over very low heat until the sugar and cocoa dissolve. Set aside and let cool to room temperature. Stir in the vanilla, whipping cream and salt.

Now shred the chocolate on a grater. Stir the shredded chocolate and the marshmallows into cocoa mix. Pour into an ice cream maker, and make ice cream according to manufacturer's directions. Be sure to stir the marshmallows and chocolate through the ice cream mix. *Serves 6–8.*

All of the following recipes can be made without an ice cream maker.

Grape-honey Yogurt Ice Cream

2 cups plain yogurt
1 6-ounce can of frozen grape juice
½ cup honey
½ cup cream

Stir the yogurt in a bowl until smooth. Then stir in the frozen grape juice, honey, and cream. Pour into a 9-inch pan. Cover with tin foil, and place in freezer until almost firm—about 2 to 3 hours. Stir a few times while freezing. *Serves 4.*

Lemon Ice Cream

1 cup whipping cream
2 tablespoons lemon juice
1 teaspoon grated lemon peel (optional)
2 egg whites
½ cup sugar

Whip the cream until soft peaks form. Mix in the lemon juice bit by bit. Add the lemon peel. Set aside. Now beat the egg whites in another bowl until foamy. Add the sugar to the egg whites and beat until stiff. Add the egg white mixture to the whipped cream mixture. Pour into a 9-inch pan, cover with tin foil, and freeze for 3 or 4 hours. Stir a few times while freezing.

Note: You can buy grated lemon peel and lemon juice in a bottle at the store. Or you can squeeze the juice and grate the peel from fresh lemons, which tastes better. *Serves 4.*

Canteloupe Ice

Here's a recipe for lovers of sherbet and fruit ice.

1 medium canteloupe
2 tablespoons fresh-squeezed lemon juice
⅓ cup honey

Cut the canteloupe in half and remove the seeds. Cut the meat of the melon off the rind and chop into bite-size pieces. Blend in a blender or food processor with the lemon juice and the honey until smooth. Pour into a 9-inch pan, and cover with tin foil. Freeze until firm, about 4 or 5 hours.

Remove from freezer. Break ice into small pieces and blend again in a blender or food processor until light and fluffy. Serve.   *Serves 4 to 6.*

Ice Cream Tortoni

This dish was invented by an Italian ice cream maker in the 1800's. It's still popular today.

1 cup crumbled macaroons
2 cups heavy cream
¼ cup confectioner's sugar
Pinch of salt
1 teaspoon vanilla extract

Set aside ¼ cup of the macaroon crumbs.

Put 1 cup of the heavy cream, the sugar and salt into a bowl. Add the remaining macaroons to the cream mixture and let them soak until they are soft.

Whip the rest of the cream. Add the vanilla. Gently fold in the macaroon mixture. Fill 8 to 10 one-half cup size paper baking cups with the mixture. Freeze. Before serving, sprinkle with the ¼ cup of macaroon crumbs.   *Serves 4 to 6.*

Baked Brownies Alaska

6 brownies (homemade or store bought)
1 pint vanilla ice cream
3 egg whites
⅛ cup sugar

Put the brownies on a baking sheet. Top each brownie with a scoop of ice cream. Place in freezer until ice cream is very firm—about 4 hours.

When you're ready to serve, preheat your oven to 450°F. Beat the egg whites with an egg beater or an electric beater until they stand in soft peaks. Stir in a little sugar and keep beating. Keep stirring in sugar until you have used the whole ⅛ cup. You will have a very stiff, sweet, white substance called *meringue* (pronounced "muh-*rang*").

Take the ice cream-brownies out of the freezer and spread the meringue over the top and sides. Cover them up completely with the meringue. Then bake in your oven for just 2 or 3 minutes, until the meringue turns light brown. Eat immediately.   *Serves 6.*

Chocolate Bananas

16 ounces of chocolate
4 bananas

Cut each banana in half and skewer each half with a wooden stick so it's like a popsicle. Melt the chocolate in a double boiler, or in a very heavy sauce pan over *very* low heat so that it melts slowly and does not burn. Let the chocolate cool 4 to 5 minutes. Then dip each banana in the melted chocolate, turning it to coat it. Put

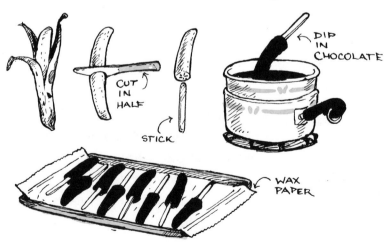

on a baking sheet, that is lined with wax paper and place in freezer. Freeze for about an hour. Remove from freezer and wait 10 minutes before serving. Wrap tightly in foil to store. *Serves 8.*

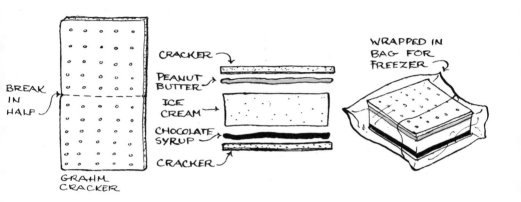

Graham Cracker Sandwiches

Thick fudge syrup
Graham crackers
Peanut butter (creamy or crunchy)
Chocolate ice cream brick (you can use any ice cream that comes in a square or rectangular package)

Put the fudge syrup in the refrigerator for at least an hour, to thicken it. Spread half the crackers with peanut butter and half with fudge syrup. Cut 1-inch slices from the brick of chocolate ice cream. Then cut the slices into squares that are the same size as the graham crackers. Place the ice cream slices on top of the chocolate fudge crackers. Top with the peanut butter crackers. Put in plastic bags, and freeze for 3 hours.

Mother Nature Parfait with Orange Sauce

Parfait is French for "perfect." Ice cream parfaits are usually made with ice cream, sauce, and fruits or nuts—all in layers.

1 tablespoon cornstarch
½ cup water
¾ cup (6 ounce can) frozen concentrated orange juice, thawed
2 pints vanilla frozen yogurt (or ice cream)

Mix the cornstarch and water in a saucepan. Blend in the orange juice, a little at a time, then bring to a boil. Lower heat and cook until thick, stirring constantly. Remove from heat and allow to cool.

Put one layer of frozen yogurt in the bottom of each parfait glass (any tall drinking glass will do if you don't have parfait glasses). Then add a layer of sauce. Repeat until your glasses are filled. Top with any of the following: orange slices, banana slices, pineapple chunks, raisins, shredded coconut, almonds, walnuts, pecans and/or peanuts, wheat germ, or granola. *Serves 8–10.*

Three Flavor Ice Cream Pie

Ice cream pies are delicious and easy to make. This one can be made with any three flavors of ice cream that appeal to you. Or you can make a pie with just one or two ice cream flavors.

1 9-inch chocolate cookie-crumb pie crust (directions on page 60)
½ pint chocolate ice cream, softened
½ cup chocolate fudge sauce (optional)
1 pint coffee ice cream, softened
1 pint vanilla ice cream, softened
Chocolate chips and whipped cream (optional)

Spoon chocolate ice cream into the crust and spread to make an even layer. Pour half of the chocolate sauce over the ice cream and spread. Put the coffee ice cream on next and top with the remaining chocolate sauce. Spread the vanilla ice cream on top of this. Freeze for at least 2 hours. You can eat the pie just like this, or top with chocolate chips or whipped cream before serving. *Makes 1 pie.*

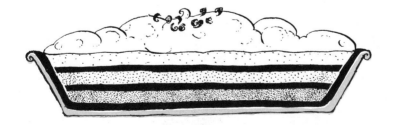

Cookie Crumb Pie Crust

1 package chocolate or vanilla wafers
½ cup margarine or butter

Preheat oven to 350°F. Crush enough wafers to make 1½ cups of crumbs. Melt the margarine or butter, cool, and add it to the crumbs a little bit at a time. Blend well after each addition. With your fingers or a wooden spoon, spread mixture into the bottom and along the sides of a 9-inch pie plate, packing it down tightly. Bake about 8 to 10 minutes.   *Makes 1 pie crust.*

Easy Ice Cream Cake

1 angel food cake (homemade or store bought)
1 quart any flavor ice cream
Whipped cream

Scoop out about half the inside of the angel food cake. Fill it with ice cream. Use the whipped cream to ice the cake and then freeze it for 2 to 4 hours. You can decorate with slices of fruit, chocolate chips, or nuts.   *Makes 1 cake.*

Acknowledgements

The author gratefully acknowledges the time and effort of: Colleen Dorfman at England Strohl/De Nigris, Sue Halls at Baskin-Robbins, Tobi Rozen at the National Association of Ice Cream Manufacturers, John Kenyon at the Ohio State University Department of Dairy Technology, Steven Mayer at Farm Foods, the makers of Soy Ice Cream, the publicity departments at Howard Johnson's, Sedutto's, Breyer's, New York Ice, Steve's Ice Cream, and the National Ice Cream Retailers' Association.

Selected Bibliography

Dickson, Paul. *The Great American Ice Cream Book.* Atheneum Publishers, 1972. New York.

Hoffman, Gar and Mable. *Ice Cream.* H.P. Books, 1981. Tucson, Arizona. Subsidiary of Fisher Publishing, Inc.

Jones, Thomas. *Ice Cream World of Baskin Robbins.* Pinnacle Books, 1975. New York.

Sherman, Steve. *The Häagen-Dazs Book of Ice Cream.* St. Martins Press, 1982. New York.

Skovol, John. "They All Scream For It!" *Time,* August 10, 1981.

Quayle, Eric. *Old Cookbooks: An Illustrated History.* Dutton, 1978, New York.

Speer, John F. "The History of Ice Cream." International Association of Ice Cream Manufacturers, Washington, D.C. 1979.

Trillin, Calvin. "American Chronicles." *The New Yorker,* July 8, 1985.

Index